George Eastman House Monograph Number **5**

Designed by John Wood

Published for Members of The George Eastman House,
900 East Avenue, Rochester, New York 14607
©1965 by the George Eastman House, Inc.
All rights reserved, Printed in the U.S.A.
Library of Congress Catalog Number 65-20164

Distributed by Horizon Press
156 Fifth Avenue, New York, New York 10010

aaron siskind *photographer*

edited with an introduction by **nathan lyons**
essays by **henry holmes smith** and
thomas b. hess statement by **aaron siskind**

george eastman house, rochester, new york

4

acknowledgments

This current monograph from the George Eastman House was prepared on the occasion of a comprehensive exhibition of Aaron Siskind's photographs which opened at the George Eastman House in March of 1965. The exhibition contained 200 photographs made between 1933 and 1963.

I am indebted to Aaron Siskind for his cooperation; to Thomas B. Hess, Executive Director of *Art News* and Mr. Henry Holmes Smith, Associate Professor of Indiana University, for their essays; and to John Wood for designing the monograph.

For their assistance in the preparation of the exhibition and the monograph, I would like also to thank the following: the Staff of the George Eastman House, with special thanks to Alice Andrews, Assistant Curator of Extension Activities, who acted as my assistant in preparing both the monograph and the exhibition; Robert Bretz, Assistant Curator of Collections, for preparing the bibliographic material; James Hilbrandt, Curatorial Assistant; and Donald Eddy, Head of Reproduction Center.

For their attention to the production of the monograph: Empire Graphics Corp., preparation of plates; Canfield & Tack, Inc., printing of plates; Rochester Typographic Service, Inc., composition; Christopher Press, Inc., printing of text section; and Riverside Book Bindery, Inc., binding.

introduction

nathan lyons

" . . . as the language of vocabulary of photography has been extended, the emphasis of meaning has shifted—shifted from *what the world looks like* to *what we feel about the world* and what we *want* the world to mean." (A. S. 1958)

In 1930 Aaron Siskind, an English teacher in New York City became interested in photography, first casually and then with a consuming intent. Stirred by the photographs on the walls of the Film and Photo League, he decided to join the group. In addition to continuing his own work he became active in arranging, installing and distributing their exhibitions. He remained with the League for three years, but left because there was, "too much doctrinairism, too little real work being done." He had already begun his document "Tabernacle City," and in 1935 began to work on the "Architecture of Bucks County."

Urged by Sid Grossman, he rejoined the Photo League in 1936 (the film group had left), and organized the Feature Group. In three years they produced a number of social documents, including: "May Day," "Harlem Document," "Dead End: the Bowery," "Portrait of a Tenement," "St. Joseph's House: the Catholic Worker Movement." The approach employed in these projects, which were widely exhibited and published, was essentially studied. Siskind commented about the nature of the documentary aproach used, " . . . Producing a photographic document involves preparation in excess. There is first the examination of the idea of the project. Then the visits to the scene, the casual conversations, and more formal interviews—talking, and listening, and looking, looking. You read what's been written, and dig out the facts and figures for your own writing. Follows the discussions to arrive at a point of view and its crystallization into a statement of aim. And finally, the pictures themselves, each one planned, talked, taken, and examined in terms of the whole. . . . " ("The Drama of Objects," *Minicam Photography,* June 1945)

His own documentation of the community of the Martha's Vineyard Camp Meeting Association (founded by Methodists in the 1830s) was achieved primarily in a study of its architecture. The community had grown from tents to little wooden cottages adorned with Gothic windows and elaborate decorative designs. Siskind was the first to do a serious study of the community. Commenting on his photographs in the introduction to the exhibition "Tabernacle City : Photographs of Aaron Siskind," (Dukes County Historical Society, Edgartown, Massachusetts, Aug. 1941) Henry Beetle Hough said, " . . . Taken over a long period of time and based upon close observation, these photographs are revealing. Their appeal to the sense of form and line excites fresh interest and can hardly fail to lead everyone interested in manifestations of folk spirit to see this American creation, this gesture of a vanished era, with altogether new eyes."

The study did include photographs of the congregational activities of the community and was approached in a traditional documentary manner. When the photographs were shown in May of that year at the Photo League, they were denounced by many of its members. Siskind had "sold out." He had turned his back on the social problems of man, the dominant preoccupation of the League at the time, and devoted his attention to a document which revealed a concern for "formal beauty." He soon left the Photo League because of what he termed, "hostility and a sense of frustration."

Returning to Martha's Vineyard in the summer of 1943, he began to make photographs on a flat plane with organic objects in geometric settings. When he eliminated deep space, he found that the objects began to take on an additional significance. His study of these photographs during the following winter encouraged him to continue. The next summer in Gloucester, the transition was evident, " . . . subject matter as such ceased to be of primary importance."

After years of documenting social realism, he now found himself in a rather unusual situation. " . . . It is a pretty uncomfortable feeling for a documentary photographer to find himself working without a plan. But the initial drive, coupled with simple, precise work habits, carried me along for a while. Then certain ideas began to emerge from the work, a predilection for certain kinds of objects, and for certain kinds of relationships. That carried me along further. . . . " ("The Drama of Objects," *Minicam Photography,* June 1945). He commented in the same article that, " . . . There are, I suppose, many ways of getting at reality. Our province is this small bit of space; and only by operating within that limited space—endlessly exploring the relationships within it—can we contribute our special meanings that come out of man's varied life. Otherwise, our photographs will be vague. They will lack impact, or they will deteriorate into just 'genre' as so many documentary shots do. . . . " He felt that in his previous work the meaning was not in the picture but in the subject photographed.

Two of Siskind's documentary photographs had been included in the Museum of Modern Art's exhibition "Image of Freedom" in 1941. In 1946, his current work was included in a second exhibition at the museum, "New Photographers." In a review of the exhibition, ("Dual Focus," *Art News,* June 1946) Beaumont Newhall quickly recognized Siskind's concern. Newhall observed that, " . . . The relation of photography to abstract art is close and challenging. The step from Janssen's macro-photographs which place emphasis on organic design to Aaron Siskind's isolation and organization within a rectangle of such apparently ungrateful subjects as a shingle or marked-up tar paper is a close one. Siskind's remark, 'I regard the picture as a new object to be contemplated for its own meaning and its own beauty,' is a point of view seldom expressed by photographers. . . . "

In 1947, with the encouragement of a friend, the painter Barney Newman, he brought his work to the Egan Gallery and held his first one-man exhibition there that year. In the years that followed he broadened his acquaintance with the New York painters and their work. Somewhat accepted by the painters, Siskind's new work found little acceptance among photographers. Two reviews of Siskind's fourth exhibition at Egan Gallery in 1951, may best point to the reaction; " . . . The current show carries to new and more confident levels Mr. Siskind's preoccupation of several years in this field. Whether this approach, which opposes a false orderliness to the impelling and inescapable 'change and disorder' of the living world, is by itself enough to fill the life of a serious photographer is certainly open to question. The doubt becomes even more insistent when one considers the fact that Mr. Siskind at one time was one of America's leading documentary photographers, in which role he was not only concerned about life but was effectively instrumental in leading others into similar directions of thinking and working photographically." (Jacob Deschin, *New York Times,* Feb. 11, 1951). And a quite similar response, " . . . Certainly it is not my province to say that he is wrong in devoting himself exclusively to the search for images in surface textures, but I would venture to say that so good a photographer ought not deliberately to stay his own growth. Siskind has the perceptive eye of the true photographer and it would be interesting if he removed the blinders that seem now to be keeping him behind a variety of obscure and obscuring walls. . . . " (Bruce Downes, *Popular Photography,* July 1951).

The art critic Elaine de Kooning, in her introduction to this same exhibition, responded to the pictures without any preconceived ideas as to what constituted the *subjects of photography.* She accepted the fact that " . . . He completely rejects whole spheres of photographic possibilities—to be found in arrested movement, dramatic subjects and the ascertainable virtuosity in recording a given view—to go looking for forms as highly personal as any that a painter could invent.

"And stubborn as a painter in the face of objective reality, he rejects the recognizable order in the large city-scenes around him to ferret out, in mystifying fragments, a more obscure scenery of his own. . . . For, selecting his images, Siskind is extraordinarily active and insistent. Although he sometimes accepts the three-dimensional compositions to be found, logically, in a grouping of solid objects—like some huge rocks in a breakwater, most of the time, he reverses the natural photographic order of vision and, through the eye of his camera, a jagged hole in a slab of concrete becomes a bulging piece of sculpture, or the grain in a plank of wood yields up rippling distances as a stretch of ocean . . . But although mood, imagery, tonalities and techniques vary from year to year, and in one show, from picture to picture, there is everywhere present a severe clarity of style through which the 'objects' that Siskind's lens creates are poignantly recognizable as his."

His involvement and conviction are stated best on his own terms and in his own words. " . . . First, and emphatically, I accept the flat picture surface as the primary frame of reference of the picture. The experience itself may be described as one of total absorption in the object. But the object serves only a personal need and the requirements of the picture. . . . " ("What is Modern Photography?" A Symposium at the Museum of Modern Art, Nov. 20, 1950.)

In 1948, he had said, "Any object, to me, is a very alive thing. In Gloucester, one summer, the rocks began to seem so animate I could hardly bear to walk over them. The previous summer I hadn't felt anything unusual about them."

For Siskind, "The start is from a previous picture. There is no preconception, rather predisposition (which predisposition includes the camera, lenses and film with me at the time). . . . The condition is total absorption: the decision (a picture!) is spontaneous. . . . Ambiguity may be the clue: there is the material, and there am I intruding my private intent. I know the imminence of the world and experience it with full sensuality; at the same time I am involved with the projection of myself as idea. Strong tensions are inevitable, pleasurable and disturbing. Is not the aesthetic optimum *order with the tensions continuing?*"

Toward this aesthetic optimum Siskind continues to work. In 1949 he resigned from public school teaching. He began to free-lance in 1950, but with little success. That same year he started teaching photography at Trenton Junior College in New Jersey one day a week; the following summer he taught at Black Mountain College with Harry Callahan. At Callahan's invitation he joined the faculty at the Institute of Design in Chicago in 1951, where he is now Head of Photography. When his first book was published in 1959, Jacquelyn Balish (then Editor of *Modern Photography*), affirmatively expressed that, " . . . He has made a giant step, taking photography out of the world where pictures and words have become interchangeable. The camera in his hands is not a literary tool, but a visual one. . . . "

N. L., 1965, Associate Director, George Eastman House

aesthetic in camera

thomas b. hess

The photographs of Aaron Siskind have long been associated with New York School Painting—the most important cultural force of the mid-century. His position is unique because Siskind has pushed photography to a point where it engages one of the most complex and mysterious issues in modern art: the ethics and aesthetics of the picture plane.

In joining cause with painting, he has sacrificed none of the camera's inherent functions as the cool witness and document *par excellence*. Perhaps due to his loyalty to the medium and its integrity, he has been able to make it prophesy many of the "looks" that have evolved out of Abstract-Expressionism—including Assemblage, Pop Art and the newest versions of Object-Art. His camera has functioned as a computer programmed with precise data on style.

Siskind's contribution was recognized from the moment of his first New York exhibition at Charles Egan's gallery in the late 1940's, where he was joined by such artists as Willem de Kooning, Reuben Nakian, Joseph Cornell, Philip Guston and Franz Kline: it was with Kline's momentous black and white images that Siskind found the closest rapport in sympathy, concept and pervading viewpoint.

The catalog to Siskind's fourth exhibition was by Elaine de Kooning, one of the most influential painter-critics of the decade, and her text placed him firmly with the new esthetic. The preface to the only previous volume of Siskind's photographs (1959) is by Harold Rosenberg (the "Apollinaire of Tenth Street") who established even stronger—if more metaphysical—links between the photographer and the best American painters. The artists invited him to join their first informal co-operative *Salon*—in an abandoned store on Ninth Street—in 1950. And although Siskind has left New York to teach in Chicago (at the Illinois Institute of Technology) for over a dozen years his presence and pictures remain as much a part of the New York scene as are the artists' all-night coffee-pots and their white-washed lofts.

The coarse, bristly texture of his imagination, his fascination with the rubble of urban living, his use of hazard and destruction as parts of the creative process, the sophisticated intellectual judgment whose pressures interpose through the chaos of his vision to fix the ultimate choices of his art, all related intimately to the aims and preoccupations of vanguard American painters. His subject matter: close-up-scapes of lichen, scaling glue, moss, cancers of grime—a whole repertory of weathered patinas—relates to the light and feel of surfaces in a painting by Franz Kline or Clyfford Still. This has long been appreciated by the artists' community.

One point crucial to Siskind's vision, however, generally has been overlooked, and it is more important than any coincidences of resemblance or echoes of "ideas in the air." Siskind has placed his medium for the first time in its history, in that ambiguous field where illusion and reality engage in endless trans-action—the picture plane, the flat surface with its dynamic tensions and interrelations.

Almost invariably, Siskind focuses his camera on a wall—a billboard in Mexico held together by layers of rotting advertising matter, the side of a henhouse or of a stone wall on Martha's Vineyard, a detail of a tenement facade. Even when he aims at the ground (a street, a beach), he will tip his camera perpendicular to the surface, which is treated as a "possible" wall. Thus the "real" view which Siskind found in nature is transformed into a plane parallel to, and at an unknown "virtual" distance behind, the glassy surface of the photographic print. Perspective, which is built-in the camera lens and which lures most photographers into *trompe-l'oeil,* is eliminated at a stroke and scale is also thrown away. It is usually impossible to tell from a Siskind photograph how large his "subject" really is or how far away the camera was placed from it. What looks like a Cyclopean wall with stones twenty feet across is an ankle-high cairn on a New England field. An enormous gesture in white on black is "really" a practice dab of housepaint. A pyramid is a toe, or vice-versa. A boy floating in the air is falling? rising? at arm's-length? 50 feet off? (On the whole, Siskind makes little things loom big—just as the memory of his images grows in your mind and you are astonished when you see them a second time; you had thought they were six feet wide, and you can hold them in your hand. This is one of the best proofs of the interior strength of his forms.)

What the artist gives you is a place (an arena) where things happen—decomposition, recrudescence, melting, congealing, pushing, slipping, fighting, mumbling—and where he has perceived that instant of poise which is the "picture." The question: "What was *really* there?" becomes as irrelevant as what Monet's lily pond *really* looked like to Mme. Monet when she rode by on her bicycle.

Obviously this connects to the experience of painters who work somewhere in the metaphysical distance between the actuality of paint-on-canvas and the illusions set up by each interacting color, line, shape. Siskind has transposed the confrontation between what palpably *is* (paper, emulsion, simulacra of nature) and what *seems* (an abstract shape, a palpable texture, a gesture you can feel through your whole arm) to his own medium. And because he respects photography's particular form of illusion, what he gains through the relative simplicity of its mechanics (and his mastery of the craft), he is apt to lose in the gap between his idea and the inhuman (mechanical) process. In other words, it may be easier for Siskind to click his shutter than it was for his friend Franz Kline to make a finishing stroke, but the painter can keep his picture there, in front of him and inside the studio, while the photograph always tends to slip away from the photographer and change itself into just another interesting, if dated, vista.

Siskind works with these possibilities. The reason he is so good is that he is constantly aware of how inevitable failure is. And here is the final paradox. As they fail as Art, the pictures that Siskind allows to come to completion rejoin life as new bits and pieces of reality—the artist's own reconstituted nature. Only through this sort of failure could Siskind triumph.

His pictures are always "straight." They have no arty shadows, he never dodges a contour—no cosmetic fuzz and no High Camp despair. It is safe to predict that Aaron Siskind will never be fashionable in the vogue bazaars. He has no irony. He is serious. His prints have the matter-of-fact, deceptively simple object-quality of, say, Shaker furniture or the Hell Gate Bridge. Their purity indicates their ethics. They also have a profundity of association and allusion, and the look of inevitability which are signs of major art.

Most photographers, longing for the Aesthetic, end up with anonymous mementoes. Art is what Aaron Siskind threw away—and art is what he is stuck with.

T. B. H., 1963-65, Executive Director, Art News

new figures
in a classic tradition

henry holmes smith

Thomas Hess, in his essay, "Aesthetic in Camera," pays tribute from the art world to Aaron Siskind's photographs: tribute, one of a number, that places Siskind's work in the small body of photography for which major artists have evinced genuine interest and enthusiasm. This said, a larger question must be faced: What is *photography's* debt to Siskind, who is now in his early sixties? It is large and to a considerable extent unacknowledged; furthermore, many photographers remain unaware that, because of Siskind's contribution, photography has finally completed its journey into the twentieth century. For, much to the joy of his friends among the artists and to the dismay of a number of photographers, Siskind has proceeded during the past twenty-five years to take up and solve some of the most difficult and tricky problems bequeathed us in the late work of Alfred Stieglitz.

Siskind, himself, in a lecture in November 1958, traced the "basic tradition for photographers today" to the work of Stieglitz after 1910. This tradition, as Siskind remarked, "involved a simple procedure and a rather uninvolved aesthetic, . . . (and) has established standards of excellence and objectivity to which we all, no matter what our particular practice, go for nourishment and discipline." Siskind described this kind of photograph as "sharp all over, . . . with a full tonal range, . . . made with the light present at the scene, . . . using the largest possible camera, preferably on a tripod, . . . the negative is printed by contact to preserve utmost clarity of definition, . . . and the look of the finished photograph is pretty well determined by the time the shutter is clicked . . . ." He called this the "classic photograph;" since it is in the "basic tradition of photography, the term "traditional" is useful in discussing this kind of camera work. It is in this sense that the term is used here. Siskind and Stieglitz, each in his own way, may be termed traditional photographers. The way their work is related, the way their contributions to the art of photography differ, and the singular importance of Siskind's work to traditional photography today are the concerns of this essay.

The work of Stieglitz paved the way for Siskind's, but it took an imagination of exceptional force to move from the Stieglitz sky pictures (his "equivalents") to the remarkable visual figures of Siskind. Two men, two separate generations of art, two different kinds of imagination were necessary. Fortunately photography shares them both. Stieglitz, however, for all his matchless accomplishments, will I think eventually be regarded less as the North Star of photography and more as a continental divide, an aesthetic watershed, on one slope the culmination of nineteenth century traditional photography and on the other the first strong suggestion of what twentieth century photography is to become. His position, and its significance in appraising Siskind's contributions, may best be examined in the light of some historical events of more than fifty years ago in which Stieglitz had a central role.

(The following account is sketched to cast light on the present, not to scoff at decisions of the past. These we must defer to, since their consequences always surround us. Must we also be reminded that hindsight illuminates brilliantly but only the past?)

Having survived a green and footless sixty-one years of the nineteenth century, unwanted and unwed to any of the other arts, photography tried to enter the twentieth century art world in disguise consisting of a faint resemblance to etchings, engravings and chalk or charcoal drawings of some of the more familiar contemporary artists of Europe and America. In 1910 photography in this attractive motley again received generous recognition as an art form at the Albright Gallery in Buffalo, N. Y. What seemed at the time a monumental victory was but the prelude to a *coup de grâce* for misplaced ambition and misunderstood success. Instead of accolades, an avalanche impended, for which the masters of 1910 were totally unprepared. The wrong art had been imitated. Small exhibitions of work by Matisse, Cézanne, Rodin, African native sculptors and Picasso at Stieglitz's 291 and elsewhere were followed by the Armory Show in February 1913, which changed completely the public notion of how broad the face of art might be. Against the work of a Cézanne or Van Gogh and the even more exasperating departures from camera vision of Matisse and Picasso, camera imitations of Cassatt or Whistler or lesser artists of that day could no longer be viewed with unqualified complacency.

Though almost everyone was aware that photography now must *do* something, they were less certain *what* it should do. As always, the problem centered on what a photographer *ought* to do with an impulse to respond to some other art. Unfortunately, the solving of this problem took a degree of sophistication supplied to few photographers. Economic and aesthetic climates have done little to encourage photographers to resort to new visual forms, although some had been uncovered incidentally by certain scientists (for example, photomicroscopists, the discoverer of Roentgen rays, and the men who had used photography to analyze animal locomotion). Small wonder that many photographers had either meager or unexercised imaginations, or that their aspirations to make art brought them to the safe ground of accepted or conventional work. Nor did such experience give much help in answering the questions raised by the shocking new art introduced in the Armory Show. Was it *really* art? If it was, and photographs were art, why did the two look so strange together? Should, could, photographs be made that would bear any resemblance to these works? None of these questions could be easily or quickly answered. Stieglitz had said that photographs should be a "direct expression of today," and amplified this suggestion by expressing admiration for the "brutally direct" work of the young Paul Strand. As late as a decade after the Armory Show, Stieglitz wrote of his sky or cloud photographs: "I know exactly what I have photographed. I know I have done something which has never been done— . . . ." No matter how one might choose to interpret such Delphic utterances, two broad courses lay open for photographers. They could study the new art for structures that were adaptable to traditional photography and incorporate these into photographs made directly from nature. Or, by one of several combinations of photographic and nonphotographic techniques, they could create a synthetic imagery (more photo-pictures than photographs) quite close in spirit to the new art, but a whole world away from traditional photography.

In the circumstances, it is remarkable that any photographer would consider either course. Photography, always a hand-me-down of the arts, had won twentieth century recognition with a bet on art that already had begun to look old fashioned. Must it now choose to gamble its small prestige by trying to resemble art forms that had aroused a storm of ridicule and rage in Europe and America? What hardihood it must have taken to wager one's time and talent at such odds. Yet some photographers did this; we have the photographs: early Strand still lifes; Coburn's Vortographs; still lifes by the elder Weston, of common household articles; by Bruguiere, of cut-out paper shapes; and geometrical compositions by Steichen, of fruit and other objects. All have an "artificial" look. After the War of 1914-1918, many artists and photographers undertook work that rested on these same impulses: photomontages by

Max Ernst, John Heartfield, George Grosz and Moholy-Nagy and a variety of work by a number of others in Dada, Bauhaus or Surrealist ranks. Judged by their photographs, the traditionalists were a serious group, and this wild new work was hardly to their taste. Most objectionable, however, was the tendency of the "photomonteurs" to cut photographs into bits which were reassembled in a totally new synthesis which could quite correctly be interpreted as an attack on the traditional spatial structures of photography.

The remarkable document "Photo-Eye," edited by Franz Roh and Jan Tschichold for the Film und Foto international exhibition in Stuttgart in 1929, shows the vigor with which these new images were produced.

(Roh's essay "Mechanism and Expression" in the same volume gives the viewpoints of thirty-six to forty-five years ago that yielded these synthetic photo-pictures. Although the translation printed here is in awkward English, the ideas will reward any reader.)

Stieglitz did not take this road. Instead, with his customary vigor, he enjoined photographers to believe in photography and avoid flim-flam, trickery and any "ism." He then set out to revitalize traditional photography, and succeeded so well that he made it look more like a new style than an old one. For those who followed him, not only was photography dragged clear out of the quicksand of imitation, but many photographers were also persuaded that a camera picture should look only like an object a camera has been pointed at. Stieglitz did not mean this; certainly his concern for contemporary aesthetic theory and his concept of equivalents bear this out, but the impression held. He also, perhaps unintentionally, appeared to support the idea that great photographs should look a good deal like nineteenth century photographs, except that the tones should be black and modulated more subtly. But most importantly, his consummate skill with structures derived from twentieth century painting elevated photography's capacity for depiction (for producing impressive descriptive illusion of an object or scene) to a high art. For this unequalled accomplishment, traditional photography is ever in his debt, and all traditional photographers who came after him have had to walk in his gigantic shadow.

Unfortunately an equally important problem remained without solution: what resources of allusion were available to traditional photography? As is true in other arts, in photography descriptive illusion is to a great extent antagonistic to allusion (that is, a reference to some object or meaning not clearly pictured). The makers of synthetic photo-pictures lacked almost all access to descriptive illusion as a unified effect, which was the great strength of traditional photography. They did have, however, an endless capacity and means for inventing allusions. The traditionalists in photography, on the other hand, rejecting utterly the resources of the makers of synthetic photo-pictures, commanded an inexhaustible supply of descriptive illusion. These two resources must be satisfactorily reconciled before photography could be used effectively as a twentieth century art. For traditional photography, which had been too mechanical, crude and truthful to fit nineteenth century art standards, would find itself too heavily burdened with descriptive illusion and too lacking in a capacity for allusion to qualify for the twentieth century. This problem was coming ever more clearly into view when, in 1937, Stieglitz for the last time laid aside his camera.

With his technical virtuosity, and the energy of his younger days, Stieglitz might have provided adequate solutions. As it was, the task fell to others, among them Aaron Siskind. From the early 1940's on, Siskind has addressed himself to the central problems of traditional photography still left unsolved. At first perhaps naively, but soon with the skill and uncanny sense of what is necessary and correct that always marks the indispensable pioneer, Siskind proceeded to provide the missing answers for which photographers, many of them without realizing it, had been waiting.

Noting that descriptive illusionistic detail, when redundant or over-precise, tends to cancel out both the strength and mystery of a figurative art, Siskind resorted to neglected methods within the scope of straightforward traditional photographic technique to restore the necessary balance between what the camera pictures and what the photographer feels. Using carefully composed details from nature, he placed descriptive illusion completely at the service of lively new figures rich with contemporary meaning.

As he continued working, Siskind also realized the exceptional clumsiness with which earlier photographers had handled allusions to the other arts. They had tried numerous devices: the directed subject clothed or unclothed, the simulated exotic costume, the simulated setting or predicament, and imitation of another way of marking, as with chalk or pencil. Based on such work, any injunction not to be influenced by the arts of painting and drawing was likely to be a doctrine less of wisdom than of despair.

Yet allusion has a peculiar power that need not be abandoned. Harold Rosenberg, in his book on Arshile Gorky, writes. " . . . art as resurrection of art gave prominence to three formal principles: allusion, parody, quotation. Of these, the first is the most profound, the true ghostly principle of historical revival, since by allusion the thing alluded to is both there and not there . . . Allusion is the basis upon which painting could, step by step, dispense with depiction without loss of meaning: on the contrary, depiction as was already well realized in the nineteenth century, could be an obstacle to communication of the artists' meaning, besides having its age-old mystery extracted by the camera . . . . "

Siskind faced up to another central problem for photography at this point: how to strike a balance between depiction, which as Rosenberg indicates had become the *assigned* task of the photograph, and allusion through which the shapes of art and nature were now capable of generating new meanings. Siskind's masterly stroke was to demonstrate, well within the limits of traditional photographic means, that what had been seen, even by a perceptive critic, only as opposing forces could be reconciled and used in photography to support one another. It thus became possible for the photographer who so desired, to place the full power of descriptive illusion (which had always been the chief public virtue of the photograph) at the service of allusion. This permitted the use of visual figures in ways analogous to the metaphors of language. As for his own work, unlike his less fortunate predecessors who had chosen to imitate the appearance of art and not its impulse, Siskind, straightforward as always, chose to base his work on an inner impulse in complete harmony with the feelings and outlook of the artists whom he knew so intimately in New York from the 1940's on. This impulse guided his eye, where many who preceded him in the years up to 1918 or thereabouts had preferred to let the eye and accepted taste control the impulse. Siskind, by his method, achieved a coincidence of image and feeling with only the simplest of technical means.

Equally important, Siskind found ways of alluding to a wide range of human experience. He did this by concentrating on the evocative forms and shapes and textures that carry for the human mind a host of inescapable associations. Thus, the event or meaning, is "both there and not there" as Rosenberg puts it. By abandoning depiction in its usual form, Siskind thus gains all the powers of suggestion. In this way he can exploit the objects of parody and quotation as well as allusion that abound in the ragtag-bobtail world of what has been worn out, lost, abandoned or misused. Here he found a host of emblems and symbols for twentieth century mankind. In a brief commentary on one of his photographs, Siskind has written: "It makes no difference what the subject matter is. The idea, the statement, is the only thing that counts . . . I care only for people—I'm interested only in human destiny. It just happens that I work symbolically—not directly with people as subjects . . . Perhaps it is that the forms, the shapes (in signs) communicate more, and are more important than what was originally said on them."

Time after time he succeeds in making the part stand for the entire event or object; the likeness of unlike objects is demonstrated with unequivocal force, the mystery of light and dark enlivens the eye and remains to haunt the mind, and the awesome forces of nature that in every instance conspire to put man in his place parade into view on surfaces where time and change have worked their surgery.

He has shown many ingenious ways to restrain the destructive tendencies of descriptive illusion, which has been a notorious destroyer of metaphorical figures in photography. Using the devices of emphasis by tone, scale or repetition and then concentrating on unexpected detail in a context for which no one else's photographs fully prepare us, Siskind adds a constant stream of new figures to replace those being worn out by the same means in the general run of photographs. We also see that Siskind has provided photography with a proper means of escape from every unreasonable restraint imposed upon it. Nineteenth century space had been forced on photography by the lenses of Paul Rudolph and his peers. Siskind exploited the detail-bearing aspect of these lenses of another day, by simply eliminating the three dimensional subject and concentrating on tone and shape and a nearly flat surface. (Hess's essay gives a superb description of this accomplishment.)

He has also demonstrated some of the ways by which the photographer may restore to traditional tonal scales the force of metaphor by exaggeration and selective emphasis. In view of all this it is not too difficult to recognize that Siskind to a large degree has been responsible for bringing photography into the twentieth century.

Whatever claims may be made for others, and there are many that can be made justly, there is available at present no comparable body of work that has addressed these problems for so long with equal attention and competence and has produced new figures so rich and various. Siskind, whose pictures embrace the concepts of reconciliation and ecological equilibrium, has discovered some of the most important means by which the traditional conventions of the camera are brought into harmony with the symbolic and pictorial needs of the present.

Of course, discoveries of this magnitude are seldom the result of an entirely rational plan. Rather, as Henry James stated, they " . . . are like those of the navigator, the chemist, the biologist, scarce more than alert recognitions. He *comes upon* the interesting thing as Columbus came upon the Isle of San Salvador, because he had moved in the right direction for it—also because he knew, with the encounter, what 'making land' then and there represented. Nature has so placed it to his profit . . . by his fine unrest . . . . "

Within a span of twelve months, the microcosm of a "picture making experience" at Gloucester in the summer of 1944 became Aaron Siskind's San Salvador. The previous summer in Martha's Vineyard he began to work on the flat plane with organic objects in geometric settings. Every day he would go out with his old familiar equipment, all of which was relatively simple. He would spend the morning exposing six films on a variety of subjects and at noon when he was finished, although he had not consciously been aware of any immense effort, he would sit down to lunch exhausted. Thus was spent the entire season.

The following summer he returned to Gloucester, only this time fresh from a task of photographing a collection of pre-Columbian sculpture for a New York exhibition. Haunted by the force of these simple shapes and rugged surfaces, Siskind found the rocks providing echoes of the sculpture. This came as revelation to a photographer who had been looking for a form as meaningful as the music he loved and the poetry he had attempted. The rock was not denied, but the echo of the artifact was strong enough to hold its own form in the rock. Day after day, impelled by this sense of discovery he returned to the subjects of the previous summer only to find they were providing him with new material. In a literal sense, his vision had been shaped by the art he had attended so closely as a photographer during the winter. He was seeing with new eyes. What he found that summer in Gloucester in the early 1940's provided firm direction for his future work. This account demonstrates the falseness of the injunction that photography is an art so unique and special that interchanges with the other arts are never to photography's advantage and must be avoided at any cost.

In this instance an overwhelming body of art work had provided him with a symbol system that completely reorganized his own vision and started him on the mature phase of his career that is sampled in the present book.

Siskind's program cannot be matched for exploration and expansion of the photographic possibilities remaining to the traditionalist. The traditional nature of his method must be emphasized because his work contains so much material that is rich and new that anyone who first encounters it may see very few connections between it and the work of Stieglitz and his direct aesthetic descendants. Yet there are several and some of them are important. Siskind has adhered strictly, almost totally, to the most rigid conventions laid down by the masters who set the style for twentieth century traditional photography: the use of a relatively large, firmly supported camera and a sharp lens; and the found object untouched, shown as it is found, where it is found. His distortions of this prescription are generally simple and available to all photographers.

By staying technically within the strictest limits of traditional photography, Siskind has demonstrated that descriptive illusion may be diverted from its age-old task in photography, where it has been slayer of metaphors. Under his guidance it has become instead foster father to a host of new figures that may yet assume all the functions of a language of the spirit.

H. H. S., February 1965, Associate Professor, Indiana University

When I make a photograph I want it to be an altogether new object, complete and self-contained, whose basic condition is order—(unlike the world of events and actions whose permanent condition is change and disorder).

The business of making a photograph may be said in simple terms to consist of three elements: the objective world (whose permanent condition is change and disorder), the sheet of paper on which the picture will be realized, and the experience which brings them together. First, and emphatically, I accept the flat plane of the picture surface as the primary frame of reference of the picture. The experience itself may be described as one of total absorption in the object. But the object serves only a personal need and the requirements of the picture. Thus, rocks are sculptured forms; a section of common decorative iron-work, springing rhythmic shapes; fragments of paper sticking to a wall, a conversation piece. And these forms, totems, masks, figures, shapes, images must finally take their place in the tonal field of the picture and strictly conform to their space environment. The object has entered the picture, in a sense; it has been photographed directly. But it is often unrecognizable; for it has been removed from its usual context, disassociated from its customary neighbors and forced into new relationships.

What is the subject matter of this apparently very personal world? It has been suggested that these shapes and images are underworld characters, the inhabitants of that vast common realm of memories that have gone down below the level of conscious control. It may be they are. The degree of emotional involvement and the amount of free association with the material being photographed would point in that direction. However, I must stress that my own interest is immediate and in the picture. What I am conscious of and what I feel is the picture I am making, the relation of that picture to others I have made and, more generally, its relation to others I have experienced.

A. S. 1950-56, Head of Photography, Institute of Design, Chicago, Illinois

Martha's Vineyard. 1954.

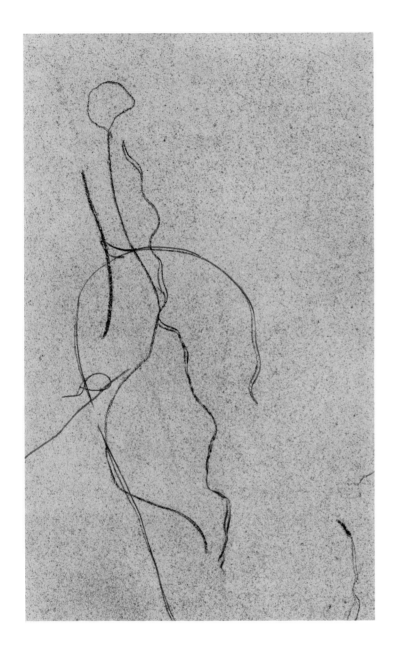

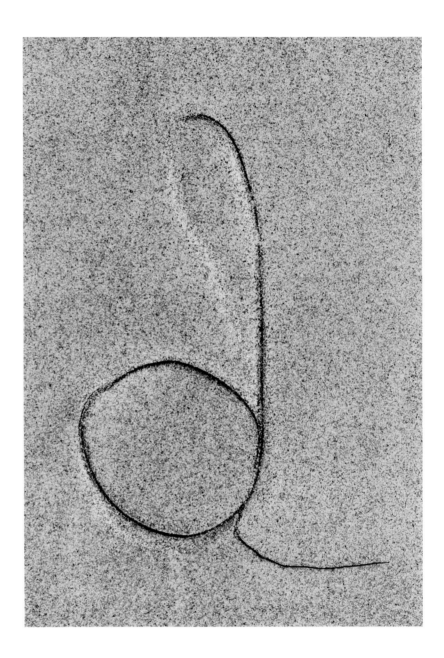

Los Angeles. 1947.

Martha's Vineyard. 1944.

Chicago Facade. 1960.

Alcoman, Mexico. 1955.

Chicago. 1957.

"Tabernacle City." 1935.

"Tabernacle City." 1935.

Chicago. 1948.

Kentucky. 1951.

Chicago. 1960.

San Luis Potosi, Mexico. 1961.

Chicago. 1960.

Chicago. 1952.

New York. 1951.

Chicago. 1960.

"Terrors & Pleasures of Levitation." 1954.   "Terrors & Pleasures of Levitation." 1954.

"Terrors & Pleasures of Levitation." 1953.

"Terrors & Pleasures of Levitation." 1954.

Rome. 1963.

Rome. 1963.

Chicago Facade. 1952.

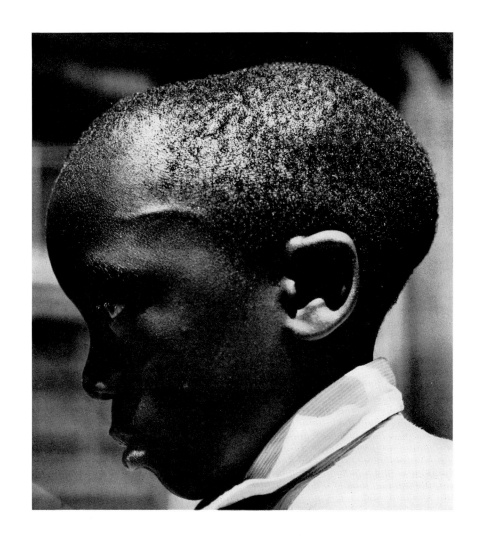

Head. 1933.

Chicago Facade. 1960.

Chicago. 1960.

Feet. 1957.   Feet. 1957.

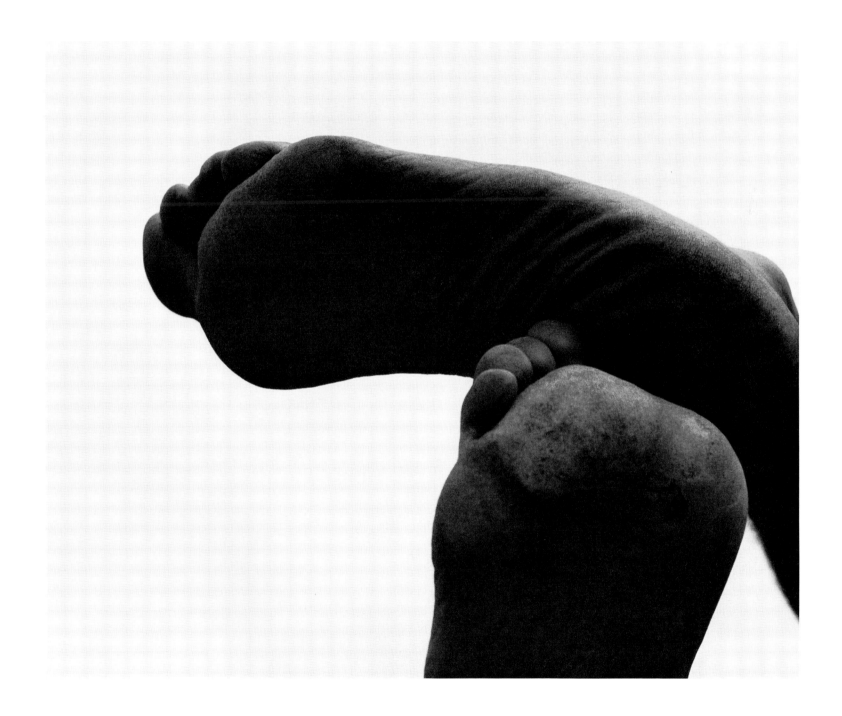

Feet. 1957.

Terracotta, Illinois. 1960.

Chicago. 1960.

Alcoman, Mexico. 1955.

Durango, Mexico. 1961.

Chicago. 1960.

Guadalajara, Mexico. 1961.

Chicago. 1957.

Chicago. 1960.

Rome. 1963.

Rome. 1963.

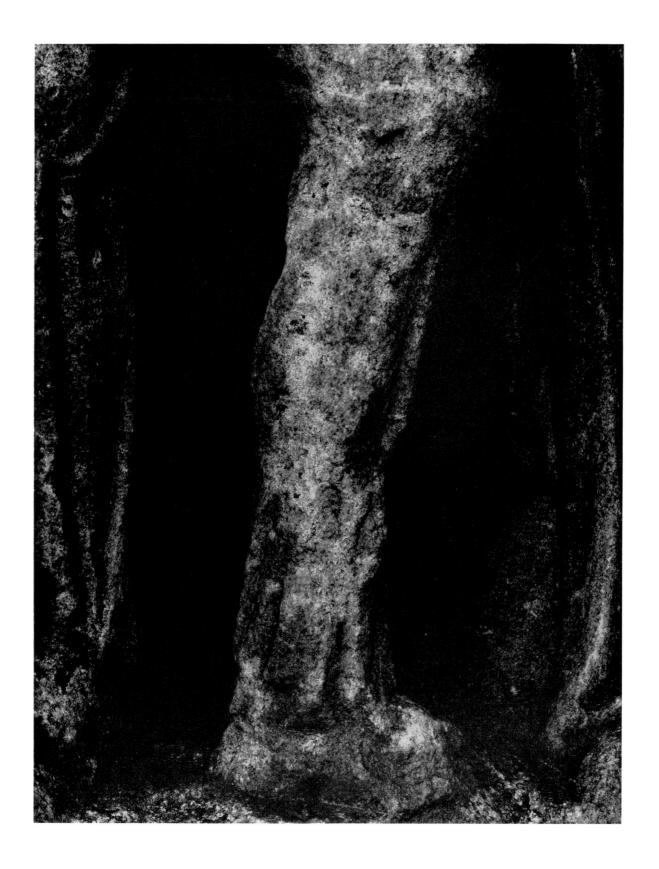

Rome: The Arch of Constantine. 1963.

Rome. 1963.

Rome. 1963.

Rome. 1963.

Rome: Appia Antica. 1963.

exhibitions 1939 PHOTO LEAGUE, New York. (Spring) 12 photographs; group exhibition.

1940 NEW YORK WORLD'S FAIR, New York. (Oct 1-15) Salon of Photography, Photographic Center, Hall of Industry & Metals. Group exhibition.

NEW SCHOOL FOR SOCIAL RESEARCH, New York. (Nov) "Harlem Document" 50 photographs by Aaron Siskind, Morris Engel, Jack Manning, Ray Corsini and others.

1941 PHOTO LEAGUE, New York. (May) "Tabernacle City" 45 photographs.

DUKES COUNTY HISTORICAL SOCIETY, Edgartown, Mass. (Aug) "Tabernacle City" 45 photographs, deposited in permanent collection after exhibition.

MUSEUM OF MODERN ART, New York. (Oct) "Image of Freedom" Group exhibition directed by Beaumont Newhall. A competition; jury for selection: Alfred H. Barr, Monroe Wheeler, Beaumont Newhall, David H. McAlpin, Ansel Adams, James Thrall Soby.

1946 MUSEUM OF MODERN ART, New York. (Spring) "New Photographers" 3 photographs; group exhibition. Directed by Nancy Newhall.

1947 EGAN GALLERY, New York. (Apr 28-May 17) 30 photographs.

ST. PAUL GALLERY, St. Paul, Minn. "The Artist, Nature and Society" 39 photographs; joint exhibition with Walter Quirt and Société Anonyme Collection.

CALIFORNIA PALACE OF THE LEGION OF HONOR, San Francisco. (Nov-Dec) 40 photographs.

1948 SANTA BARBARA MUSEUM OF ART, Santa Barbara, Calif. (Jan) 40 photographs.

DELAWARE GALLERY, New Hope, Pa. (Feb) "Old Houses of Bucks County" 45 photographs completed and prepared for publication in 1945; exhibition deposited in Bucks County Historical Society, Doylestown, Pa., 1948.

BLACK MOUNTAIN COLLEGE, Black Mountain, N. C. (Mar) 40 photographs.

EGAN GALLERY, New York. (Spring) 30 photographs.

MUSEUM OF MODERN ART, New York. (Apr 6-Jul 11) "In and Out of Focus" 4 photographs; group exhibition.

QUEENS COLLEGE LIBRARY, Flushing, N. Y., 25 photographs.

PHOTO LEAGUE, N. Y. "This is the Photo League" 2 photographs; group exhibition. Also included a display of documentary work of the Feature Group.

1949 EGAN GALLERY, New York. (Jan 4-21) 30 photographs.

INSTITUTE OF DESIGN, Chicago, Ill. 40 photographs.

1950 MUSEUM OF MODERN ART, New York. (Aug 2-Sep 17) "51 American Photographers" directed by Edward Steichen.

1951 EGAN GALLERY, New York. (Feb 5-24) 30 photographs.

SEVEN STAIRS GALLERY, Chicago, Ill. (Feb 29-Mar 29) 30 photographs.

MUSEUM OF MODERN ART, New York. (May 2-Jul 4) "Abstraction in Photography" 3 photographs; group exhibition. Directed by Edward Steichen.

"NINTH STREET SHOW," New York. Group exhibition of painters; Aaron Siskind only photographer invited to participate.

BLACK MOUNTAIN COLLEGE, Black Mountain, N. C. (Summer) 40 photographs.

MUSEUM OF MODERN ART, New York. (Nov 30-Jan 6) "Photographs as Christmas Gifts" group exhibition.

1952 PORTLAND MUSEUM OF ART, Portland, Ore. 40 photographs.

MUSEUM OF MODERN ART, New York. (Nov-Mar 1953) "Diogenes with a Camera, II" 25 photographs; group exhibition with Ansel Adams, Dorothea Lange, Tosh Matsumoto, Todd Webb. Directed by Edward Steichen.

MUSEUM OF MODERN ART, New York. (Aug 6-19) "Then (1839) and Now (1952)" group exhibition.

1953 MUSEUM OF MODERN ART, New York. "Contemporary American Photography" group exhibition for the International Program.

1954 EGAN GALLERY, New York. (-Jun 12) 60 photographs.

MENEMSHA GALLERY, Martha's Vineyard, Mass. (Aug) 40 photographs.

GEORGE EASTMAN HOUSE, Rochester, N. Y. (Nov) 65 photographs. Directed by Minor White.

1955 NORTHWESTERN UNIVERSITY, Evanston, Ill. 60 photographs. Directed by Tom Foldes.

DENVER ART MUSEUM, Denver, Col. (Oct-Nov) 50 photographs.

ART INSTITUTE OF CHICAGO, Chicago, Ill. (Nov 15- Jan 1, 1956) 30 photographs. Directed by Peter Pollack.

SANTA BARBARA MUSEUM OF ART, Santa Barbara, Calif. (Dec-Jan 1956) 40 photographs.

1956 UNIVERSITY OF KENTUCKY, Lexington, Ky. (Jan) "Creative Photography—1956" 10 photographs; group exhibition. Directed by Van Deren Coke.

CINCINNATI ART MUSEUM, Cincinnati, Ohio. (Mar-Apr) Exhibition for Contemporary Art Center; 35 photographs.

EVANSTON TOWNSHIP HIGH SCHOOL, Evanston, Ill. (May 26-Jun 8) 50 photographs.

POSNAN, POLAND. 40 photographs.

1957 AMERICAN FEDERATION OF ARTS, New York. (Oct 1957-Oct 1958) "Abstract Photography" traveling exhibition; included photographs by Harry Callahan, Art Siegal, Art Sinsabaugh, Aaron Siskind. Organized by Aaron Siskind.

UNITED STATES DEPARTMENT OF STATE. 50 photographs by Harry Callahan and Aaron Siskind shown at U.S. Information Centers in Paris, Algiers and London.

1958 INDIANA UNIVERSITY, Bloomington, Ind. (Spring) "Coke Collection" 2 photographs in exhibition of 122 photographs by 21 photographers.

ALFRED UNIVERSITY, Alfred, N. Y."Aaron Siskind: Photographs" from the collection of John Wood.

SAN FRANCISCO STATE COLLEGE, San Francisco, Calif. 40 photographs.

MUSEUM OF MODERN ART, New York. (Nov 26-Jan 18, 1959) "Photographs from the Museum Collection"

4 photographs; group exhibition.

1959 MARTHA JACKSON GALLERY, New York. (Feb 9-20) 23 photographs.

CORNELL UNIVERSITY, Ithaca, N. Y. (Spring) Art Festival. 12 photographs. (The only photographs included among other arts.)

NEW YORK COLISEUM, New York. (Spring) "Art: USA: 59" 3 photographs; group exhibition.

INDIANA UNIVERSITY, Bloomington, Ind. "Photographer's Choice" 3 photographs; group exhibition. Directed by Henry Holmes Smith.

CARL SIEMBAB GALLERY, Boston, Mass. (Oct) 20 photographs.

MUSEUM OF MODERN ART, New York. "Toward the New Museum of Modern Art—A Bid for Space, Part I" group exhibition.

HOLLAND-GOLDOWSKY GALLERY, Chicago, Ill. (Nov) 20 photographs.

GEORGE EASTMAN HOUSE, Rochester, N. Y. (Nov-Dec) "Photography at Mid-Century" (Tenth Anniversary Exhibition) 253 photographers in group exhibition; later shown at Walker Art Gallery (Minneapolis), M. H. DeYoung Memorial Museum (San Francisco), Wadsworth Atheneum (Hartford), Addison Gallery of American Art (Andover), Museum of Fine Arts (Boston). Organized by Beaumont Newhall, Walter Chappell, Nathan Lyons.

1960 LIMELIGHT GALLERY, New York. (Jan 19-Feb 29) "Photographs by Professors" photographs by Lou Block, Van Deren Coke, Allen Downes, Walter Rosenblum, Aaron Siskind, Minor White. Directed by Lew Parella.

MUSEUM OF MODERN ART, New York. (Feb 17-Apr 10) "The Sense of Abstraction" 7 photographs; group exhibition. Directed by Grace Mayer and Kathleen Haven.

NEWARK MUSEUM OF ART, Newark, N. J. (Apr) 3 photographs; group exhibition.

THE CLIFF DWELLERS, Chicago, Ill. (May) Harry Callahan and Aaron Siskind, courtesy of Holland-Goldowsky Gallery, 25 photographs each.

ART CENTER OF NORTHERN NEW JERSEY, Englewood, N. J. (Sep) 3 photographs.

MUSEUM OF MODERN ART, New York. (Oct 2-16) "Photographs for Collectors" group exhibition.

1961 KALAMAZOO INSTITUTE OF ARTS, Kalamazoo, Mich. (Feb) "Three Photographers" Wynn Bullock, Aaron Siskind (29 photographs), David Vestal.

GEORGE EASTMAN HOUSE, Rochester, N. Y. "The Art of Photography" a permanent exhibition. 3 photographs. Directed by Nancy Newhall.

KALAMAZOO INSTITUTE OF ARTS, Kalamazoo, Mich. (Sep) "Twentieth Century American Art; Painting, Drawing, Sculpture, Photography" 2 photographs.

CLEVELAND INSTITUTE OF ART, Cleveland, Ohio. (Nov 13-Dec 1) Photographs by Ansel Adams, Nathan Lyons, Aaron Siskind, Minor White. Directed by Emilio Grossi.

1962 DE CORDOVA MUSEUM, Lincoln, Mass. (Jan 28-Mar 18) "Photography-USA; National Invitational Photography Exhibition" 68 photographers represented by approximately 460 photographs.

SCHUMAN GALLERY, Rochester, N. Y. (Apr 16-May 12) "10 Photographers" photographs by Ansel Adams, Wynn Bullock, Harry Callahan, Paul Caponigro, Walter Chappell, Syl Labrot, Nathan Lyons, Aaron Siskind, Minor White, Tom Muir Wilson. Directed by Nathan Lyons.

MUSEUM OF MODERN ART, New York. "Toward the New Museum of Modern Art—A Bid for Space, Part III" group exhibition.

JOHN GIBSON GALLERY, Chicago, Ill. (Apr 20-May 17) 35 photographs. (6 were 50 x 50 inch enlargements.)

VII PHOTOGRAPHERS' GALLERY, Provincetown, Mass. (Jun 15-Sep 30) 10 photographs.

HANAMURA'S, Detroit, Mich. (Oct 14-?) Two-man exhibition with Toshiko Takaezu.

GEORGE EASTMAN HOUSE, Rochester, N. Y. (Dec 12-

68

Jan 15, 1963) "Exhibition and Print Sale" 2 photographs; group exhibition. Directed by Nathan Lyons.

1963 UNIVERSITY OF ILLINOIS, Urbana, Ill. (Mar 3-Apr 7) "Six Photographers" 10 photographs each by Berenice Abbott, Len Gittleman, Ray Metzker, Nathan Lyons, Aaron Siskind, Edmund Teske. Directed by Art Sinsabaugh.

GEORGE EASTMAN HOUSE, Rochester, N. Y. "Aaron Siskind" 25 photographs; traveling exhibition.

MINNEAPOLIS INSTITUTE OF ARTS, Minneapolis, Minn. (Nov 26-Jan 19, 1964) "A Century of American Photography" 1 photograph; group exhibition.

1964 ART INSTITUTE OF CHICAGO, Chicago, Ill. (Mar 14-Apr 19) 35 photographs from 1954 to 1964. Directed by Hugh Edwards.

MUSEUM OF MODERN ART, New York. (May 25) The Edward Steichen Photography Center. Initial installation, group exhibition. Directed by Grace Mayer.

MUSEUM OF MODERN ART, New York. (May 25-Aug 23) "The Photographer's Eye" 1 photograph; group exhibition. Directed by John Szarkowski.

BOSTON ARTS FESTIVAL, Boston, Mass. (Jun 16-Aug 9) 15 photographs; invitational group exhibition. Directed by Carl Siembab.

NEW YORK STATE EXPOSITION, Syracuse, N. Y., in collaboration with the George Eastman House. (Sep 1-7) "Photography 64 / An Invitational Exhibition" 5 photographs; group exhibition. Later shown at Mobile Art Gallery, Museum of Fine Arts (Houston), Harper College (Binghamton, N. Y.), University of Nebraska, North Carolina State University at Raleigh, University of Florida, Phillips Exeter Academy (Exeter, N. H.), Akron Art Institute, Indiana University, Mankato State College (Mankato, Minn.). Directed by Nathan Lyons.

NEW YORK WORLD'S FAIR, New York. (Oct) "Contemporary Photographs from the George Eastman House Collection, 1900-1964" 1 photograph; group exhibition. Shown at the George Eastman House, Jan 22-

Mar 7, 1965. Later shown at Wells College (Aurora, N. Y.), Baltimore Museum of Arts, Southern Vermont Art Center (Manchester), M. H. De Young Memorial Museum (San Francisco), University of Hawaii, Boise Art Association (Boise, Idaho), Wabash College (Crawfordsvills, Ind.), Massillon Museum (Massillon, Ohio). Directed by Nathan Lyons.

ROSE ART MUSEUM, BRANDEIS UNIVERSITY, Waltham, Mass. (Oct) "The Painter and the Photograph" later shown at Indiana University, State University of Iowa, Isaac Delgado Museum of Art (New Orleans), University of New Mexico, Santa Barbara Museum of Art. Organized by Van Deren Coke.

STATE UNIVERSITY COLLEGE, Buffalo, N. Y. (Nov 9-Dec 4) "Thirty Photographers" 4 photographs. Directed by Oscar Bailey and Charles Swedlund.

KRANNERT ART MUSEUM, UNIVERSITY OF ILLINOIS, Urbana, Ill. "Purchase Award Photographs from the Krannert Art Museum" traveling exhibition; Photographs by Berenice Abbott, Harry Callahan, Robert Frank, William Garnett, Len Gittleman, Nathan Lyons, Ray Metzker, Wayne Miller, Aaron Siskind, Edmund Teske.

MICHIGAN STATE UNIVERSITY, East Lansing, Mich. (Dec 28-Jan 17, 1965) 49 photographs.

1965 UNIVERSITY OF WISCONSIN-MILWAUKEE SCHOOL OF FINE ARTS GALLERY, Milwaukee, Wis. (Mar 2-26) "Exhibition 11/10" 21 photographers including Aaron Siskind.

POMONA COLLEGE, Claremont, Calif. (Mar 10-Apr 4) 45 photographs.

GEORGE EASTMAN HOUSE, Rochester, N. Y. (Mar 26-May 21) "The Photographs of Aaron Siskind" 200 photographs; scheduled to circulate. Directed by Nathan Lyons.

MANKATO STATE COLLEGE, Mankato, Minn. (Apr 6-30) 49 photographs.

bibliography

CHAPPELL, WALTER. Review of *Aaron Siskind: Photographs,* by Aaron Siskind, *Image,* v.9, n.2 (Jun 1960) p.99-101.

COKE, VAN DEREN. "The Art of Photography in College Teaching," *College Art Journal,* v.19, n.4 (Summer 1960) p.332-42. (Cover photograph by Siskind)

COSS, BILL. "Aaron Siskind: Humanity in Abstraction," *Metronome,* v.78, n.1 (Jan 1961) p.18-20. (Transcript of conversation between Bill Coss, Herb Snitzer and Dave Heath; two photographs by Siskind)

DE KOONING, ELAINE. "The Photographs of Aaron Siskind," typescript introduction to the 1951 exhibition at the Egan Gallery.

DESCHIN, JACOB. "New Studies by Siskind," *New York Times,* Sunday, June 6, 1954, p.x13 (Review)

———. "Siskind's World; Strange Pictures Found on Decayed Surfaces," *New York Times,* Sunday, Feb 11, 1951, p.x13 (Review)

———. "Museum Exhibit Connects Photography and Truth," *New York Times,* Sunday Nov 30, 1952, p.x15 (Review)

———. "Two Ways of Seeing," *Modern Photography,* v.15, n.5 (May 1951) p.22. (One photograph by Siskind)

DOWNES, BRUCE. "Let's Talk Photography," (regular column) *Popular Photography,* v.29 n.1 (Jul 1951) p.22. (Review)

GROSSI, EMILIO. "On the Art of Photography," *Fine Arts,* v.8, n.390 (Nov 19, 1961) p.5 (Introduction to exhibition at Cleveland Art Institute)

HESS, THOMAS B. "The Walls: Aaron Siskind's Photography: A Cross-Section," *Portfolio,* n.7 (Winter 1963) p.64-71, 108-109. (Seven photographs by Siskind; portrait)

HOUGH, HENRY BEETLE, and ALEX R. STAVENITZ. "Tabernacle City . . . Some Observations, Historical and Critical," (four-page leaflet printed for Exhibition *"Tabernacle City: Photographs by Aaron Siskind,"* August, 1941)

LIPPMANN, MINNA. "Chilmark Summer Visitor Expresses Abstract in his Unusual Photographs," *New Bedford Standard Times,* Sep 4, 1948.

LOGAN, JOHN. "Eight Poems on Portraits of the Foot," in his *Spring of the Thief,* New York, Knopf, 1963, p.47-50.

————. "On a Photograph by Aaron Siskind," *Chicago Choice,* n.1 (1961) p.68-69. (Later included in his *Spring of the Thief,* New York, Knopf, 1963, p.41)

————. "A Suite of Six Pieces for Siskind," in his *Spring of the Thief,* New York, Knopf, 1963, p.44.

NEUGASS, FRITZ. "Aaron Siskind," *Camera,* v.32, n.1 (Jan 1955) p.2-11. (Ten photographs by Siskind, with an interpretation by Dr. Neugass)

NEWHALL, BEAUMONT. "Dual Focus," *Art News,* v.45, n.4 (June 1946) p.36-9, 54. (Review of two exhibitions: "New Photographers," at Museum of Modern Art, and membership exhibition at Society of Photographic Illustrators; one photograph by Siskind)

————. *The History of Photography from 1839 to the Present Day.* (4th edition, revised and enlarged) New York, Museum of Modern Art, 1964. (Two photographs and quotation by Siskind, p.199)

————. "Photographing the Reality of the Abstract," *New Directions,* n.15 (1955) p.161-171. (Illustrations include three photographs by Siskind)

OERI, GEORGINE. "Aaron Siskind: 'Abstract' Photography," *Graphis,* v.7, n.37 (1951) p.354-57. (Four photographs by Siskind with text in German, English, French)

PARELLA, LEW. "Photographs by Professors," introduction and notes for an exhibition at the Limelight Gallery, January 19 to February 24, 1960. (Exhibition catalogue)

POLLACK, PETER. "Aaron Siskind," introduction to an exhibition at the Art Institute of Chicago, November 15, 1955 to January 1, 1956. Chicago, Art Institute of Chicago, 1955. (Announcement)

————. "Callahan and Siskind—The Magic of the Commonplace," chapter 33 in his *Picture History of Photography* . . . New York, Abrams, 1958, p.432-434, 444-445. (Illustrations include eight photographs by Siskind)

ROSENBERG, HAROLD. "Aaron Siskind: the Camera and Action Art," *Art News,* v.58, n.5 (Sep 1959) p.22-23. (Three photographs by Siskind and reprint of Rosenberg's introduction to *Aaron Siskind: Photographs*)

————. "Aaron Siskind," *Perspective on Ideas and the Arts,* v.11, n.10 (Oct 1962) p.40-47. (Eleven photographs by Siskind, including cover, with reprint of introduction to *Aaron Siskind: Photographs*)

————. "Aaron Siskind—Photographs," *Graphis,* v.16, (May 1960) p.262. (One photograph with brief text in German, English, French)

SISKIND, AARON. "Accidents of time . . ." Quoted in "This is my best . . ." *Art Photography* (Jun 1954) p.16-19. (With six photographs and portrait by Callahan)

————. "Credo 1950," *Spectrum,* v.6, n.2 (May 1956) p.27-28. (Two photographs by Siskind included elsewhere in this issue)

————. "The Drama of Objects," *Minicam Photography,* v.8, n.9 (Jun 1945) p.20-23. (Five photographs including self-portrait by Siskind)

————. "The Essential Photographic Act . . ." *Art News,* v.54, n.8 (Dec 1955) p.36-37. (Twelve photographs by Siskind with statement. The statement was reprinted in the catalogue of the exhibition *Three Photographers,* Kalamazoo Institute of Arts, 1961)

————. "It Makes No Difference . . ." In the article "Where I Find My Pictures," *Modern Photography,* v.22, n.2 (Feb 1958) p.75. (One photograph by Siskind)

————. "Learning Photography at the Institute of Design," (by Aaron Siskind and Harry Callahan) *Aperture,* v.4, n.4 (1956) p.147-149.

————. "Notes on the Photographic Act," *Spectrum,*

v.6, n.2, (May 1956) p.26.

———. *Aaron Siskind: Photographs*. With an introduction by Harold Rosenberg. New York, Horizon Press, 1959. (Fifty photographs by Siskind)

———. "Photography as an Art Form," Unpublished lecture delivered at the Art Institute of Chicago, Nov 7, 1958.

———. Review of *The Decisive Moment*, by Henri Cartier-Bresson, *Saturday Review* (Dec 20, 1952) p.14.

———. "When I make a photograph . . ." Statement prepared for a Symposium at the Museum of Modern Art, quoted in Walter Rosenblum's "What is Modern Photography—A Symposium at the Museum of Modern Art, Nov 20, 1950," *American Photography,* v.45, n.3 (Mar 1951) p.146-53. (Also quoted: statements by Margaret Bourke-White, Ben Shahn, Irving Penn, Wright Morris, Charles Sheeler, Homer Page, Gjon Mill, Walker Evans, Lisette Model, Edward Steichen's introduction. Illustrations include one photograph by Siskind)

SMITH, HENRY HOLMES. "Image, Obscurity and Interpretation," *Aperture,* v.5, n.4 (1957) p.136-47. (One photograph by Siskind)

———. "Photographer's Choice," introduction and notes for an exhibition at Indiana University, with statements by several of the exhibitors, published in *Photographer's Choice,* n.1 (Spring 1959), issued as the catalogue of the exhibition.

———. "Photography in Our Time; A Note on Some Prospects for the Seventh Decade," *Three Photographers,* the catalogue of an exhibition at the Kalamazoo Institute of Arts, Feb 5 to Mar 3, 1961, published in Bulletin n.2 (Feb 1961) of the Kalamazoo Institute of Arts.

STEICHEN, EDWARD. "The New Selective Lens; Younger American Photographers Enter the Collection of New York's Museum of Modern Art," *Art News,* v.49, n.5 (Sep 1950) p.22-25. (Two photographs)

TIMBERMAN, ELIZABETH. "Aaron Siskind," *Photo Notes,* n.d. (ca.Jun 1948) (Review)

WHITE, MINOR. Review of *Aaron Siskind: Photographs,* by Aaron Siskind, *Aperture,* v.7, n.3 (1959) p.123-124, 126. (One photograph by Siskind)

———. "On the Strength of a Mirage," *Art in America,* v.46, n.1 (Spring 1958) p.52-55. (Illustrations include one Siskind photograph)

WILLIAMS, JONATHAN. "Aaron Siskind / Eight Signs," *Black Mountain Review,* n.5 (Summer 1955) p.77-78. (Poetry accompanied by eight photographs by Siskind)

WILSON, HILDA LOVEMAN. "Aaron Siskind," typescript introduction to the 1948 exhibition at the Egan Gallery.

———. "The Camera's New Eye," *Mademoiselle* (Dec 1947) p.154-155, 201-203. (Two photographs by Siskind)

PHOTOGRAPHS HAVE APPEARED IN THE FOLLOWING: PUBLICATIONS

COKE, VAN DEREN. *The Painter and the Photograph*. Albuquerque, The University of New Mexico Press, 1964, p.50 (Exhibition catalogue; one photograph by Siskind)

JANIS, HARRIET, and RUDI BLESH. *Collage*. Philadelphia, Chilton, 1963. (Illustrations include two photographs by Siskind)

Masters of Modern Art. Edited by Alfred H. Barr, Jr., New York, Museum of Modern Art, 1954. (One photograph by Siskind)

Modern Artists in America, First Series. (By Robert Motherwell and others.) New York, Wittenborn and Schultz, 1951. (Frontispiece and installation photographs)

Photography at Mid-Century. Tenth Anniversary Exhibition. With an introduction by Beaumont Newhall. Rochester, N. Y., The George Eastman House, 1959. (Exhibition catalogue; one photograph by Siskind)

Poet's Camera. Selection of photographs by Bryan Holme; selection of poetry by Thomas Forman. New York, American Studio, 1946, pl.56. (One photograph by Siskind)

A Selection of Works of Art From the Art Collections at the University of Nebraska. Lincoln, Nebraska, The University, 1963. pl.92. (Exhibition catalogue) (One photograph by Siskind)

Six Photographers—1963. An Exhibition of Contemporary Photography. Urbana, College of Fine and Applied Arts, University of Illinois, 1963, p.34 (Exhibition catalogue; two photographs by Siskind)

Twentieth Century American Art; Painting, Drawing, Sculpture, Photography. An exhibition on the occasion of the opening of the new Art Center Building, Sept 1961. Kalamazoo, Art Center of the Kalamazoo Institute of Arts, 1961. (Exhibition catalogue; one photograph by Siskind)

PERIODICALS

Aperture. v.4, n.1 (1956) p.14. (One photograph by Siskind with statement in "Creative Photography—1956" by Van Deren Coke)

Aperture. v.5, n.3 (1957) p.112-130. (Five photographs by Siskind; five readings by Kurt Safranski, Henry Holmes Smith, Myron Martin, Walter Chappell, Sam Tung Wu, in "The Experience of Photographs.")

Architectural Forum. v.101, n.4 (Oct 1954) p.128-133. (Nine photographs by Siskind and Alvin Loginski, James Blair, Richard Nickel, Asao Doi, Len Gittleman, in "Chicago's Sullivan in New Photographs.")

Art International. v.4, n.2/3 (1960) p.73.

Big Table. v.1, n.3 (1959) (Four photographs plus cover photograph—all from "The Terrors and Pleasures of Levitation" series.)

Casabella. n.204 (Feb/Mar 1954) p.7-29. "The Architecture of Louis Sullivan." (With Hugh Duncan and students of Institute of Design)

Chicago Review. (Spring 1958) p. 64-65. (Two photographs by Siskind)

Craft Horizons. v.22, n.3 (May/June 1962) p.18-21. (Seven photographs, one by Siskind, from project conducted at Institute of Design, Chicago, under direction of Siskind, with excerpts from Ralph Marlowe Lines' introduction to Dover edition of Sullivan's *Autobiography of an Idea,* in article "Louis H. Sullivan, 1856-1924.")

————.v.22, n.3 (May/June 1962) p.22-25. (Five photographs by Siskind in portfolio "Nature as Artist; Five Photographic Studies by Aaron Siskind.")

Fortune. v.9, n.2 (Feb 1934) p.29. (First Siskind photograph reproduced in a magazine in article "State Housing: American Style.")

————. v.20, n.1 (Jul 1939) p.78-79. (Three photographs by Siskind, others by Hansel Mieth, Wendell MacRae, Carl Mydams, Pictures, Inc., from "Harlem Document.")

Graphis, v.19 (Jul 1963) p.293. (One photograph by Siskind in F. Berrer's "The Expressive Potentialities of Photography")

Industrial Design. v.1, n.4 (Aug 1954) p.100-104. (Six photographs by Siskind, introduction by Alvin Lustig, in "Photographs by Aaron Siskind.")

Photography of the World. v.3. Tokyo, Heibonsha Ltd., 1958. p.11-15. (Five photographs in this annual of photography)

Popular Photography. v.12, n.3 (Mar 1943) p.47. (One photograph by Siskind)

Time. v.62, n.18 (Nov 2, 1953) p.58-74. (One photograph by Siskind in "Half a Century of U. S. Photography."

Town and Country. (Jun 1936) "Country Auctions."

U. S. Camera Annual. (One photograph each in 1937, 1941, 1947, 1949, 1951, 1957)

chronology

1903 Born in New York City, December 4th.

1926 Received Bachelor of Social Science degree from The College of the City of New York. Began teaching English in New York City public schools. Chief interests in college: literature and music.

1930 First experience with a camera on trip to Bermuda.

1932 Active interest in photography. Purchased 9 x 12 cm Voigtlander Avis camera. Learned to process and print. Stirred by photographs on walls of Film & Photo League and joined the group. Active in arranging, installing and distributing their exhibitions.
Began work on "Tabernacle City" document.
Left Film & Photo League after three years.

1935 Began work on "Architecture of Bucks County" document.

1936 Rejoined Photo League at request of Sid Grossman.
Organized Feature Group (Morris Engel, Jack Manning, Ray Corsini and others). Group worked for three years producing "Harlem Document," "Dead End: the Bowry," "Portrait of a Tenement," "St. Joseph's House: the Catholic Worker Movement."

1939 Produced document "Most Crowded Block in the World."

1941 Exhibited "Tabernacle City" document at Photo League. Left the League shortly thereafter.
First exhibition at Museum of Modern Art, "Image of Freedom." (group exhibition)

1943 Summer on Martha's Vineyard; began to work on flat plane with organic objects in geometrical setting.

1944 Summer in Gloucester important for development of what had begun previous summer on Martha's Vineyard; subject matter as such ceased to be of primary importance.

1945 Summer in Gloucester.

1947 First exhibition at Egan Gallery. Broadened acquaintance with New York painters and their work. Siskind's work somewhat accepted by artists—practically no acceptance by photographers.

Visited Edward Weston briefly in California. (A friend had brought him to visit Siskind in New York the previous year where he had seen some of Siskind's photographs.

1948 Visited Chicago; met Harry Callahan.

1949 Six months sabbatical leave from teaching. Went West in Model A Ford; spent some time with Fred Sommer in Arizona.
Resigned teaching position in September.

1950 Free-lanced with little success. Taught photography at Trenton Junior College one day a week.
Participated in symposium, "What is Modern Photography?", Museum of Modern Art.

1951 Summer, taught photography at Black Mountain College with Callahan.
September, began teaching at Institute of Design, Illinois Institute of Technology, at Callahan's invitation.

1952 Directed advanced students at Institute of Design in development of definitive study of architecture of Adler and Sullivan.

1955 Summer in Mexico.
Prepared and participated in traveling exhibition "Abstract Photography," for American Federation of Arts.

1957 Participated in an exhibition with Harry Callahan for U. S. Department of State, shown in U. S. Information Centers in Paris, Algiers, London.

1959 Publication of first book *Aaron Siskind: Photographs,* New York, Horizon Press.

1961 Appointed Head of Photography, Institute of Design, Illinois Institute of Technology.
Summer in Mexico.

1962 Co-editor of *Choice* (a magazine of poetry and photography).

1963 Four months in Italy, seven weeks in Greece.
Founding member of Society for Photographic Education.

1964 Member of the Board of Trustees of the Gallery of Contemporary Art, Chicago, Illinois.